BEAVERS
Dam Builders

Lynn George

PowerKiDS press
New York

Published in 2011 by The Rosen Publishing Group, Inc.
29 East 21st Street, New York, NY 10010

First Edition

Editor: Joanne Randolph
Book Design: Kate Laczynski
Photo Researcher: Jessica Gerweck

Photo Credits: Cover, pp. 1, 14–15 © Bernd Zoller/age fotostock; back cover and interior graphic © www.iStockphoto.com/Branko Miokovic; p. 4 Eastcott Momatiuk/Getty Images; pp. 5, 14 (beaver, top left) © www.iStockphoto.com/kawisign; p. 6 (left) Kevin Moloney/Getty Images; p. 6 (right) © www.iStockphoto.com/imagegrafx; p. 7 Alan and Sandy Carey/Getty Images; p. 8 (left) Sven Zacek/Getty Images; p. 8 (right) Ron Spomer/Getty Images; pp. 9, 16, 18–19, 20, 22 Shutterstock.com; pp. 10–11, 13 © Lynda Richardson/Peter Arnold, Inc.; p. 12 Altrendo Nature/Getty Images; p. 14 (hard hat) © www.iStockphoto.com/Don Nichols; p. 14 (beaver lodge) Dorling Kindersley/Getty Images; p. 17 Bob Bennett/Getty Images; p. 21 Norbert Rosing/Getty Images.

Library of Congress Cataloging-in-Publication Data

George, Lynn.
  Beavers : dam builders / Lynn George. — 1st ed.
      p. cm. — (Animal architects)
  Includes index.
  ISBN 978-1-4488-0698-0 (library binding) — ISBN 978-1-4488-1357-5 (pbk.) — ISBN 978-1-4488-1358-2 (6-pack)
  1. Beavers—Habitations—Juvenile literature. I. Title.
  QL737.R632G45 2011
  599.37—dc22

                                    2010008871

Manufactured in the United States of America

CPSIA Compliance Information: Batch #WS10PK: For Further Information contact Rosen Publishing, New York, New York at 1-800-237-9932

CONTENTS

MEET THE BUSY BEAVER

Almost everyone knows that beavers have brown fur, flat tails, and live in water. Did you also know that they are natural **engineers**? Beavers change their **environments** more than any animal except people. They are almost always working. That is why people say "busy as a beaver."

Here you can see a beaver chewing on a stick. Beavers' front paws have five fingers with long claws used for digging and other work.

There are two kinds of beavers. The American beaver lives in North America. The Eurasian beaver lives in Europe and Asia. Beavers are very large **rodents**. They might even be bigger

than you. A beaver can be up to 4 feet (1 m) long, including its tail. It can weigh up to 80 pounds (36 kg)!

THE BEAVER'S SPECIAL BODY

A beaver's tail is covered with thick, scaly skin. The tail can be up to 1 foot (30 cm) long.

Like those of other rodents, beavers' front teeth are always growing. Their teeth get worn down as the beavers chew through trees and eat bark.

Beavers are well **adapted** for their lives in the water. They are well adapted for cutting down trees, too. Beavers have paddle-shaped tails and **webbed** back feet for swimming. Beavers can close their ears, noses, and parts of their mouths behind their teeth to keep water out.

The beaver's flat tail is great for swimming. The beaver also uses it to slap the water to tell other beavers there is danger. On land, the tail helps the beaver stand up while chewing through trees.

The beaver's front teeth are very long and hard to help it cut trees. The matter that makes its teeth hard also makes them orange!

WATER AND WOODS

Beavers eat grasses and parts of a tree's bark, as the two beavers above are doing. They also eat other plants.

Beavers live in streams, rivers, ponds, **marshes**, and along the shores of large lakes. Beavers need trees to build their famous **lodges** and dams. For this reason, they live in bodies of water in forests. Trees also supply beavers with some of their food. They eat leaves, tiny branches, and the inner

Here is a tree that has been cut down by a beaver. A beaver cannot move a large tree like this in one piece. It must first cut it into smaller logs with its teeth.

bark. They like willows and other trees with soft wood. They also eat roots, grasses, water plants, and fruit. The food beavers eat is hard to digest.

Luckily, they have help! Tiny living things live inside their bodies and help them break down their food.

Beavers store branches under the water to eat during winter. They can also live off fat stored in their tails during the cold winter months.

BEAVER FAMILIES

You likely live at home with one or more parents and maybe brothers and sisters. Young beavers do, too. Babies, called kits, are born in the spring. They start swimming within one day of being born. They drink milk from their mothers for up to three months. Then they eat plants, just as adults do. When they are one year

old, they start helping their parents work on the lodge and build dams. They also help care for the new kits born that year.

When beavers are two years old, they leave home to find a **mate**. Mates stay together for life. They will build their own lodge and start a family.

HOMES THAT ARE HARD TO REACH

Beavers live with their families in homes, called lodges. These homes are hard to reach. Beavers often build their homes in the middle of lakes or ponds. The entrances are under the water. This makes it hard for enemies to get to beavers. On the outside, the lodge may look like a pile of sticks. It is strong and carefully built, though.

It takes beavers about three weeks to build a lodge. The

This beaver lodge is in Miner Lake, in Montana. Some beaver lodges may be up to 10 feet (3 m) tall. Most are about 3 feet (1 m) tall.

space inside is above the water and stays comfortable and dry. An opening in the top lets in fresh air.

Beavers sometimes live in deep dens along the shore instead of lodges. A family may have several lodges or dens. They pick one to stay in during the winter.

INSIDE VIEW:
BEAVER LODGES

1 The lodge is built of sticks, bark, plants, and rocks. The beavers then cover it with mud to seal it. That keeps it dry and comfortable inside.

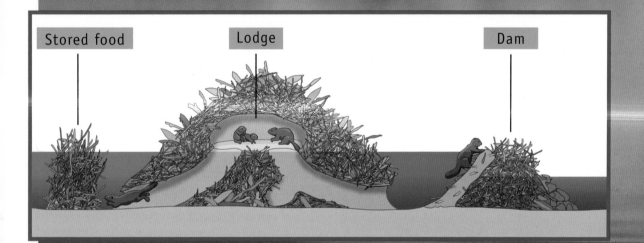

Stored food   Lodge   Dam

8 A tunnel may lead from the main room to a nest room. This is where the kits are born. It is smaller than the main room.

7 Inside the lodge is a large main room about 6.5 feet (2 m) long and about 2 feet (61 cm) high. Beavers cover the floor with plant matter.

2 Beavers start a lodge by jabbing sticks into the mud to form a base. Then they pile more building matter on top of that until the lodge is large enough.

3 Using their strong teeth, beavers cut down small trees for their lodge. It takes a beaver about 20 minutes to cut down a tree that is 6 inches (15 cm) wide.

4 Beavers pull the cut trees or float them on water to get them to the lodge. To carry the mud, beavers hold it against their chests with their front paws.

5 Most lodges are 10 feet (3 m) high and 20 feet (6 m) wide at the base. However, some are almost two times that size!

6 Beavers are always working on their lodges. They mend them and add to them. The lodges grow larger over time.

WHY BEAVERS BUILD DAMS

Beavers are even more famous for their dams than for their lodges. Why do they build dams, though? Dams block streams and rivers and form still, deep ponds. Why would a beaver want that? Beavers need ponds to make the right **habitats** for their homes. Ponds make safe places for lodges that

It may take a beaver family a week to build a 35-foot-(11 m) long dam. Beavers need deep ponds so all the water will not turn to ice in the winter.

enemies cannot reach. Beavers' favorite plants also grow in ponds.

Beaver dams are engineering wonders. They are built with the same simple matter used

for lodges, yet they turn small rivers or streams into large ponds. Dams come in many sizes. The largest ever recorded was 2,140 feet (650 m) long and 14 feet (4 m) high!

HOW BEAVERS BUILD DAMS

Have you ever seen a beaver dam? It may not look like much, but building one takes great skill. Just as they do when they build lodges, beavers first cut down trees then cut the trees into logs. Next, they must get the logs to the dam. Sometimes they pull them. However, it is easier to float them in water. Beavers often dig **canals** to move logs.

Logs and stones form the dam's base. Then rocks, logs,

Do you see the beaver dam at the bottom of this picture? Once the dam is built, beavers make their habitat even bigger by digging canals to reach new trees.

and plant matter are piled on top. Mud holds everything together. You might think the beaver spreads the mud with its flat tail. This is not true, though. Beavers spread mud on the dam with their feet and noses. Now the dam is done!

Beavers may build more than one dam in their habitat. They check the dams often for holes and fix any problems as soon as they find them.

ARE DAMS GOOD OR BAD?

You might wonder what happens when a pond suddenly appears in land that did not have one before. This is a good question. These engineering wonders sometimes cause problems. Dams change habitats. Sometimes plants and animals that once lived in a place can no longer live there. Dams can cause floods that hurt farmland, homes, roads, and forests.

Beavers are not thinking about whether cutting down trees and building dams will help or hurt their surroundings. They are just trying to make a habitat for themselves.

A beaver can cut down up to 200 trees a year to build dams and lodges and to use as food. Beavers make new homes for many animals that need wetlands to live, though.

Beaver dams also do much good. They make **wetlands**. Many kinds of animals and plants need wetlands and would disappear without them.

Wetlands can also keep floods from happening because they take in lots of water. They help stop **erosion**. They can also clean water so it is safer for plants, animals, and people!

BEAVERS IN THE WORLD

When settlers first came to North America, beavers were everywhere. There may have been as many as 400 million. That is more beavers than there are people in the United States today!

By the early 1900s, beavers had almost completely disappeared. People hunted them for food and for their **pelts**. People killed beavers because they did not like beaver dams and the way that they changed the land.

Later, people learned about the good effects of beaver dams. They worked to care for beavers and keep them safe. Today, there are about 10 million beavers in North America. We must continue to value these natural engineers.

GLOSSARY

adapted (uh-DAPT-ed) Changed to fit requirements.

canals (ka-NALZ) Waterways made by people or animals like beavers.

engineers (en-juh-NEERZ) Masters at planning and building things.

environments (en-VY-ern-ments) All the living things and conditions of places.

erosion (ih-ROH-zhun) The wearing away of land over time.

habitats (HA-buh-tats) The places where animals or plants naturally live.

lodges (LOJ-iz) Homes for certain animals.

marshes (MAHRSH-ez) Areas of soft, wet land.

mate (MAYT) A partner for making babies.

pelts (PELTS) Animal skins with the fur still on them.

rodents (ROH-dents) Animals with gnawing teeth, such as mice.

webbed (WEBD) Having skin between the toes, as ducks, frogs, and other animals that swim do.

wetlands (WET-landz) Lands with a lot of wetness in the soil.

INDEX

WEB SITES

Due to the changing nature of Internet links, PowerKids Press has developed an online list of Web sites related to the subject of this book. This site is updated regularly. Please use this link to access the list:
www.powerkidslinks.com/arch/beaver/